Finding Our Way Back to Ourselves

Healing Our Past and Finding Inner Peace

Stella Georgiou

First published by Busybird Publishing 2021

Copyright © 2021 Stella Georgiou

ISBN
Print: 978-1-922465-49-8
Ebook: 978-1-922465-50-4

This work is copyright. Apart from any use permitted under the Copyright Act 1968, no part of this publication may be reproduced, stored in a retrieval system or transmitted in any form or by any means, electronic, mechanical, photocopying, recording or otherwise, without the prior written permission of Stella Georgiou.

Cover design: Busybird Publishing
Layout and typesetting: Busybird Publishing

Busybird Publishing
2/118 Para Road
Montmorency, Victoria
Australia 3094
www.busybird.com.au

Dedicated to my precious children Anadele, James and Nicole my grandchildren Xavier and Indy and my soul child Kira.

You make my world a better place and I love you all more than all the stars in all the galaxies.

My amazing friends, you are my chosen family my world is solid because of you!

Contents

The Purpose of This Book   1

Chapter 1
  Fear Driven Parenting   9

Chapter 2
  Creating Experiences to Match Our Beliefs   35

Chapter 3
  Suffering is the Absence of Self Love   49

Chapter 4
  Shifting From Victim to Power   63

Photos   74

Chapter 5
  Let Go and Grow   87

A Poetic Reflection   95

About the Author   109

Recommended Resources   111

Notes   117

The Purpose of This Book

"It's never too late for a new beginning in your life."

– Joyce Meyers

Hello beautiful soul,

Are you ready to leave the hurts of your past behind you where it belongs? Are you willing to allow yourself, to live a life filled with peace, joy and happiness?

I want to share with you how trauma, values and beliefs, formed through my eyes as a child, affected all areas of my life. For many years I suffered from self-doubt, physical and emotional pain which stopped me from reaching my full potential. In the process of writing my story I had many conversations with family members about my childhood. During these discussions I gained deeper insight into the subject of perception and how we each experience the same events differently.

My curiosity about perception led me down the path of both perception and memory. Although how we perceive and human memory makes us who we are, these are complex processes that researches are still trying to better understand.

What we do know is that during our formative years, between the ages of one to nine, we form our values and beliefs about ourselves and the world. As children we learn most of our values from our parents and extended family.

We learn whether the world is a safe place and whether we are loved, who loves us, what happens when we cry or laugh and much more. Our brains develop connections faster in the first five years than any other time in our lives.

This is the time when the foundations for our life are laid down, how we learn, our health and how we behave. We then go out into the world where everyone else is doing the best they can with what they know. When our values are simply inherited from the people around us and do not truly align with who we are and our life purpose then things feel wrong. Life feels uneasy. We feel out of touch, disconnected, restless and unhappy. We find ourselves looking for people and things outside of ourselves to make us happy.

Like so many, I wasn't aware of how my past experiences were affecting my life and how they were the root cause of my unhappiness. I hadn't discovered who I was at my deepest nature, not who I thought I had to be in order to fit in or gain the love and approval of others. I had read about it, but somehow, I wasn't able to apply this into my own life. That is until the painful experiences in my life forced me to seek a new way of being. Often it is these painful or extremely uncomfortable feelings that drive us to make changes. I now understand that experiences can either make or break us. Only through awareness, courage, curiosity, wisdom, forgiveness and an open heart and mind are we able to learn and to grow from all our experiences.

Living a life of joy, peace and happiness is possible for you too. For as long as we are breathing it is *NEVER* too late to start again! Finding happiness does, however, require a commitment to continue to learn and grow. No one can stop you from learning a little every day to develop the skills you need to find the peace and happiness you are looking for. But no-one can do it for you, only you can help yourself grow into who you want to become. As children we may not have had choices. As adults we have a choice to learn and to grow from our experiences or to stay stuck, we just can't choose both.

These days I am more in touch with myself and my own needs. I live by values that serve me, without judgement of myself or others and from here I am in a much better place to connect. I no longer need to prove myself right or to please others.

Thank you for being here and may what I share encourage you to pursue the happiness that is your birth right so that you too can enjoy all of life's riches.

Chapter 1

Fear Driven Parenting

There I was, centre of attention, in my pretty white dress and ready for another performance, all eyes on me as my mother's words echoed, "She's so clever". The apple of my mother's eye, I was her sixth child from a family of seven children and I adored her. I would always seek to be by her side, sit close to her even if I sat on the floor right up against her legs, so that I could feel the warmth from her body.

My sister who was almost ten years older than me, played a big part in my upbringing, as a toddler I often called her mum. A child herself, one day she dressed me so that our brother could take me to Mum's work. When we arrived, Mum noticed I wasn't wearing any underwear. This was just one of many minor mishaps given that children were left to care for children. My parents owned the local cafe and worked long hours leaving the older children in charge at home. Mum and Dad had made many sacrifices to establish themselves in Cyprus only to leave it all behind like many who migrated from war-stricken countries.

My family's first attempt to immigrate to Australia was in 1965. This was short lived as my father became ill and so we went back home. We returned to Australia in 1970 when I was nine years old, due to the continuing threat of imminent war with Turkey. My father was 47 years old and Mum was 45 with five children ranging between the ages of 19 and 5. In August 1974 Turkey invaded Cyprus and the people of our village were forced to leave their homes.

Until this day the situation in Cyprus remains unresolved.

When we arrived in Australia in 1970 we lived in a share house with another family until my parents purchased a small two-bedroom house in Northcote. This modest home accommodated our family of seven with myself and four other siblings sharing a room. This purchase along with our application for Australian Citizenship signified the beginning of our new life.

My parents worked long hours sewing for an employer from the garage in our backyard. Most days they would work from sunrise until late at night to re-establish themselves. One day I became unwell and my parents were unaware until they found me unconscious. I was admitted to hospital in a coma and diagnosed with sepsis and bacterial meningitis. My parents were advised that my condition was critical and my chances of survival were low. If I did recover there was a high chance of permanent brain damage. When I eventually regained consciousness, I had lost my sight and memory. My father was devastated, telling Mum that if these symptoms were permanent he intended to kill me and himself as he couldn't bear this outcome. Fortunately I made what appeared to be a full recovery. It was a lengthy hospital stay which required a private room where I was isolated from other patients due to the contagious nature of my illness. I had never been away from my family, being alone made me feel scared and anxious.

When I was discharged from hospital I overheard my parents discussing their concerns over having to pay the huge hospital expenses and I ran out of the room crying. I was so distressed knowing that I had added to my parent's financial burdens, I promised to one day repay them. When I was fourteen years old I applied for a part time job at the local Woolies store. I felt tremendous guilt as I could see that my parents were struggling financially and so I worked whenever I was offered a shift and paid for my schoolbooks, uniform and anything else I needed.

After my illness I had difficulty with comprehension which affected my learning, I didn't know how to express this to my teachers or my family. I struggled through school and often had nightmares of failing exams. I eventually dropped out of school at age seventeen to start a career in the banking industry. I felt anxious yet optimistic at the opportunity to provide for myself financially and no longer having schoolwork to worry about.

Although I found most subjects difficult to grasp I have always had a passion for expression both written and verbal. I was inspired to write poetry when I was in my early teens. My first memory of writing was when I first started sneaking around with George, my first boyfriend. George would later become the father of my three beautiful children and eventually my ex-husband. My parents were very strict and I was not allowed to have friends let alone a boyfriend. Writing allowed me to express my feelings in ways I was otherwise not able to do. I had a book of verses where I felt free and safe to express myself. George was the bass guitarist in a high school band, and I wrote songs that he had written music to. I gave my book of verses to him when he was putting music to my words. One day I asked him for the book and he told me he had thrown it out.

At about the same time my sister had found my diary and read it. I was so afraid that my sister would tell our parents about what she had read about me and George. I felt that my life was not worth living, as I had no doubt my father would kill me. This may seem an overreaction but if you are a child raised in a home where violence is a way of discipline and control, then you would understand my fear. I was so scared I wanted to end my life, rather than face the wrath of my father. I locked myself in our laundry too scared to come out. I knew Dad had poison stored on the top shelf, so I found myself with the bottle in my hand intending to end my life. In that moment I felt that was the only way out of this situation. Fortunately for me, my fear of ending my life was larger than my fear of my father and I couldn't do it.

I am not sure if it was because George threw away my book of verses or the fear of what could have happened if my sister had exposed to my parents what she read that made me stop writing. That was over forty years ago.

Growing up I don't remember getting affection. My mother herself didn't have her parents as role models as her father passed away when she was very young. My grandmother was advised to place my mother and her brother in an orphanage as she wasn't able to provide for them. Mum's grandfather would visit her regularly but her mother only visited once a year due to the lack of public transport available in those days. My mother's only brother was placed in a different orphanage and so they became estranged during their childhood.

When Mum was seventeen years old her grandfather arranged for her to be married. In the absence of her parents in her upbringing Mum didn't learn the necessary skills to become an effective parent. My father was responsible for the discipline in our home and affection did not come naturally to him either. As humans we are hardwired to need love and in its absence I learned to be an attention seeker and a people pleaser in order to get the attention I needed.

My parents did not know how to love me because of who I was but for what I did.

If I disappointed them that love would be withdrawn as a way of punishing me, to force me to toe the line. I was therefore clueless about what constitutes emotional give and take or the nature of healthy relationships. My parents would reward me with approval for being the daughter they wanted rather than the person I was. I felt unworthy of love so as an adult I searched for approval in others.

When I started working I feared that others would see me as my parents saw me and as I saw myself: not good enough. Being raised in a family where we were constantly compared and criticised, triggered feelings of shame at being exposed as deficient. Constantly living in a state of stress both at work and at home eventually took its toll on my health.

About two years after I commenced work in the bank I found myself in a doctor's clinic with chronic Repetitive Strain Injury. My arm was placed in a plaster cast and I was advised to rest. As I had learnt to place my self worth on what I achieved, I continued to work placing added stress to my arm. Eventually this would extend to both arms and my condition became chronic. Despite my employer providing various treatments and therapies my condition continued to deteriorate. I became an inconvenience to my doctor and my employer as my condition was not improving and a psychiatric assessment was requested. The medical report concluded that my pain was psychosomatic. I was asked about my personal life and in particular, my childhood. I can remember saying, 'I was a happy child' and I honestly believed that. That is not to say that I had not experienced trauma, rather a reflection of my personality. I look for the best in others, I am also an empath which makes me more sensitive to the emotions of those around me. I would always seek to make others smile, especially my mother as she had plenty to worry about and I didn't want to add to that. What I didn't realise was that whatever happens in our mind also happens in our body. In my case as I was sensitive to the emotions of others I was dealing with not only my emotions but those of people around me and this was having an effect on my health.

Screaming matches, verbal abuse and violence was how my family communicated. Being raised in this kind of environment left me feeling scared and helpless.

In my professional life I was a dedicated, honest, loyal and hardworking employee and was promoted very early on in my career. I received many accolades and much recognition for my dedication and excellent work. My peers looked up to me, I was the go-to person in my workplace. The pain I felt in my body was real, I had physical symptoms: swelling of my wrist and bruising through my fingers – yet I felt that my employer doubted my suffering. How could they doubt my integrity?

Why were they trying to blame my pain on something other than what it was? Why was no-one acknowledging my pain? I didn't understand why I was being treated so badly, why didn't anyone care? I was suffering and yet I couldn't make sense of any of it. Upon reflection I was scared that my employer was no different to my parents, withdrawing approval when I was not performing in a way they had become accustomed to.

My health was not improving. Desperate to get relief from my unbearable physical and emotional pain I began to wonder why my doctors were asking about my past. I started to question everything in my life. I questioned my own thoughts, my actions and behaviours, not understanding why all this was happening to me caused me anxiety and further added to my health problems. I needed to dig deep, it was messy trying to unravel the parts of me I myself didn't even understand. It felt like I was going through an identity crisis as I tried to work out who I really was, and who I wanted to become.

I began to realise that I was living my entire life in the way my parents thought I should. Deep down I knew that if I didn't, they wouldn't love me and so I struggled between trying to gain their love and approval and being true to myself. This extended to my work life as I often worked without breaks to meet unrealistic expectations. Everything I did was according to my parents rules and anything I wanted to do was done in shame, guilt and secrecy.

When I was twenty-one I married George; I thought that was the only way to escape my home life and start again. He didn't treat me very well, yet my mother shamed me into marrying him as I had slept with him. Could this be the cause of my physical pain? I began to raise the issues I was not happy about in our marriage. He resented my suggestion that my ill health could be related to our relationship and told me that I was crazy. I later realised that he was even more troubled than I was. When I tried to reach out to my family, my mother's advice was, "Go back to your husband". There seemed no way out, everywhere I turned I hit a brick wall. Although I was now an adult I continued to live by values and beliefs I had formed as a child and I still needed my parents love, acceptance and approval. I honestly didn't know how I could escape this destructive pattern which continued to affect my life.

I didn't understand how my childhood could affect the relationship I was in now or how it could have anything to do with what I was experiencing. How could memories buried deep inside, values and beliefs we form as children affect us later in life? That was all in the past, or so I thought. Like the time my father tied up our dog, shot him, and burnt him in a barrel. I will forever have the vision of the charred body of our dog. We relied on the animals we had for food and the dog had killed our rabbits. Dad said that because he had the taste of blood, he had to be put down. Fifty years ago, this was just what the people did in the small village in Cyprus where we lived. As a very young child I was traumatised by what I saw. I couldn't understand Dad telling me that he loved the dog, yet he didn't hesitate to kill him.

Political unrest in Cyprus was ongoing during my childhood. In the sixties someone had written the words "Communists" in great big writing on the bitumen road outside our home. I guess as children we would have been exposed to discussions regarding politics. My girlfriend and I used chalk to write the words, "You are mistaken" alongside this comment.

This resulted in my family being held responsible for the comments. My father was interrogated by the authorities. Our comments were seen as seditious literature, which carried heavy penalties of up to two years imprisonment. If it were not for my father's good standing in our community the consequences could have been severe.

My father assumed that my sister, who was six years older than me, was responsible for the comments. I remember a vision of my sister coming home from a walk; she had been out collecting wildflowers with her friend. It was a beautiful sunny afternoon and as she innocently walked into our back yard, without asking if she was responsible for the comments, our father whipped her using electrical wire. I watched in horror, too afraid to own up to the fact that my friend and I were responsible. The beating was so severe she still wears the scars on her back.

Physical abuse at the hands of our father was not new to her. Unlike me, she was stubborn and this often got her into trouble with Dad. As a child when my mother asked her, "Who do you love the most?" She would reply, "The one that hits me." Our mother found humour in this, perhaps it was because she could relate.

There are also many memories of my father beating Mum, threatening to kill her. Hunting knives, cleavers, carving knives and machetes were a part of daily life and Dad owned many of these. He would threaten to cut our mother's throat or the tongue out of her mouth to silence her. My mother has always been a very strong, outspoken woman, and this would often get her into trouble as my father tried to control her. My father's threats toward her terrified me and caused me much anxiety and fear.

This was my mother's second marriage. My father supported her to leave her first husband who abused and neglected her and their two children. Dad developed an affection for her and wanted to rescue her. She had no family support as she and her husband had migrated to Cyprus from Egypt.

Dad believed that he had rescued her from her past and she should be eternally grateful to him. He treated her like he owned her. The truth is he rescued her from one type of abuse and introduced her to another. He also had another emotionally damaging condition for rescuing her, which was to leave her two young children behind. Mum said that she always believed that he would eventually change his mind about the children but he never did. She became estranged from her children until her ex-husband challenged her. They eventually were forced to take one of the children. My step-brother came to live with us and he would become a victim of my father's bitter resentment, harsh discipline and cruelty.

The more my father rejected him the more my brother craved his approval. Dad described him as the product of "bad seed" and that he would never amount to any good. Understandably, my brother battled with depression for most of his life.

My father himself also paid a high price for choosing to be with my mother. As she was a married woman with two young children, his family did not approve. Dad's family tried hard to convince him to leave her but once he made a promise to her he could not go back on his word. Because of this my father's family disowned him and excluded him from the family inheritance. Dad's mother did however give him a parcel of land, which was filled with rocks. My father was an extremely hard-working man; he and Mum removed the rocks one by one and built a huge water tank to collect rainwater.

They would later use the rainwater to plant a citrus orchard on what was once barren land. Dad had very little education as he had only completed grade three but he was an incredibly resourceful man and achieved many things in life. My father had many great qualities, he was a hard-working honest man who made many personal sacrifices to financially support his family. He was a shy, private man of few words who had high expectations of himself. His downfalls were his inability to effectively manage his emotions and his tragic way of expressing his needs. This led to his physical and emotional abuse toward the people he loved and who loved him. His other downfall was the fact that his fear of judgement and his pride would not enable him to accept anyone who did not fit inside his model of right and wrong, good or bad. Values and limiting beliefs he had learned from his family and carried throughout his lifetime and the judgements he placed on himself and others.

During my journey of self-discovery, the empath in me had a burning desire to reconnect with my step-brother and sister. In 2006 I travelled to Cyprus to convey my message to them, that my father was no different to his own children. I wanted them to know that the way he treated them was nothing to do with them not being his own. The moment my sister and I laid eyes on one another, there was an instant connection. I could see our mother in her eyes, she welcomed me and my family into her home with a wonderful home cooked meal.

Food was how our mother showed her love for us, so this felt like home, I felt as though I had always known her. She told me that she had forgiven our mother for leaving her behind, she was curious about the sort of person our mother was. She soon realised that the life we lived was more troubled than her own. The one thing we shared was the stigma of being the children of a woman who ran off with another man.

When I returned from my trip, I reconnected our mother with my stepsister. My father was not happy about this, but despite his reaction I couldn't help but notice that he had leaned over in his chair to catch a glimpse of the photos I had brought home.

Growing up, something I had learned about my father was he was a man of his word. Once he had made a decision about something, he would never go back on his word, even if he regretted it.

Our Values form the foundation of our lives, they dictate the choices we make and determine the direction of our life.

What values were you raised with?

Do your values bring you happiness?

These are questions that you must ask yourself if you are to find meaning, happiness, success and connection in life.

Chapter 2

Creating Experiences to Match Our Beliefs

During puberty I went from a happy, confident, bubbly little girl, to a young girl who lacked self-confidence. I wore loose clothing, as I was embarrassed of my changing body. I became very self-conscious and did everything I could to avoid criticism. I witnessed how my father used physical abuse to control our family and so I learned to lay low and toe the line. Despite this, I craved his love so I would follow him around the house, seeking his attention and validation. I also learned that making my mother proud would mean she would boast about me which boosted my confidence and made me feel special. Because of this I was drawn to her.

Learning to gain love and approval by living by the expectations of others spilled out into the rest of my life and affected my career, my relationships and every other area of my life. I can remember feeling physically ill if someone criticised me in any way, if I made a mistake, or if my environment was not neat and tidy, if all was not perfect. It was only a matter of time before this would spiral out of control.

This amount of stress to control everything eventually starts to affect both our internal and external world. As long as I could avoid criticism I felt worthy. I would say to people, I feel really lucky, anything I strive for I achieve. I thought achievement was a way of proving our self-worth. What I couldn't see was that because of my fear of rejection, this created an obsessive nature. Striving for perfection in every area of life is, as you can imagine, an exhausting, unsustainable task. This led to feelings of hopelessness and depression and yet

I had learned at a young age to do whatever it took to avoid criticism. This was a cycle I was on for many years. I didn't understand that battles should be chosen carefully, and only if they take us toward our goals and our life purpose. Achievement has nothing to do with self-worth.

Dedication, ongoing commitment and hard work are what enables our goals to be achieved. And I am a dedicated, committed and hard working person, and therefore I achieved whatever goals I set myself. What I was not aware of was, who's goals were they? Whose values and beliefs were tied into my goals. And what did my goals and achievements have to do with my self-worth? The only time I felt worthy or that I was enough was when I was living up to other people's expectations. The emptiness inside of me was always alive and I didn't understand why. I had not done the deep work necessary to discover my own life purpose. I was living by inherited values and beliefs which didn't serve me. It is a profound moment in all of our lives when we can let go of control and surrender to something bigger.

Growing up I always remember trying to fit in. When I was in high school most of the girls had boyfriends. I didn't want to be different so I told them that I had one too. I made up an imaginary one and I called him Peter.

My parents were very strict, I was not allowed to go out and I attended an all-girls' school so I had no access to boys. There was a boy who lived directly across the road from our home. He became friends with my brother; they would often play cricket. They wouldn't let me bat and would only let me play if I fetched the ball for them. I spent many afternoons chasing the ball for them so I could hang out with them.

The boy's name was George, I have mentioned him earlier in my story, he was reserved and always smiling. I recall he called me honey one day, the fact that he noticed me caused me to be instantly drawn to him. I didn't feel attractive. Well in reality I felt ugly, so much so that I would scratch my face out of photos in our family album. I think this is because my father would tease me and call me black face. Upon reflection I now see that he meant this in an affectionate, playful way. Perhaps it was because I was not used to getting his attention or my sensitive nature but as a child it made me feel ugly. So the fact that George had noticed me, was a new experience for me. I held onto the hope that he would like me, and so I did whatever it took to make sure he did. At age fifteen my friend Patty started dating George's best friend, and I think because of this, he asked me to be his girlfriend.

Patty and I would sneak around to meet with the boys, and as you can imagine in my quest to be liked, I gave up my virginity to him. Eventually my mother realised that I had been secretly spending time with George. She warned me that if I had sex with him, I would have to marry him, as no one else would have me. Now, there's a *limiting belief!* One that caused much of my unhappiness and heartache. I was very close to my mother. For me, her word was gospel. She constantly praised me and would often tell people how clever I was. She placed me on a pedestal and I became her golden child. I didn't realise the heavy burden of responsibility that was attached to this.

Later in life I came to realise that my relationship with my mother was a complicated one. I remember a time I had spent the day with George and my mother found out. She told my father. When I came home they both confronted me and questioned where I was. Afraid to tell them the truth I said I had been at work. My father hit me across the face so hard with the back of his hand that I was thrown across the room. I could hear my mother in the background shouting, "hang her". I was in disbelief that the mother who I thought loved me, wanted me dead. I was scared and wanted to pack my clothes and leave but I had nowhere to go. I had no life experience and even though I felt trapped I didn't know how I would survive without my family. I didn't understand any of it. I just felt shame, guilt, fear, trapped and helpless.

My relationship with George was just as troubled as my other relationships. He constantly broke up with me, and I kept running back to him as my mother's words, "no one else will have you" rang in my ears.

Deep down I knew that marrying George was a mistake and I know that he did too. His mental health issues became more evident to me once we lived together but this was my life and I was determined to make the most of my situation. The stress of it all started to affect my health and my doctor told me that sometimes having a baby helps. He wasn't aware of my personal problems as I only ever discussed my health with him. I had always wanted a family so I thought that perhaps things would get better if I had a baby to love.

We fell pregnant to our first child. When I told George the news he walked out of the room and didn't react. George had difficulty showing me affection yet this felt normal to me as my parents were very much the same. During my pregnancy he showed very little interest in my growing belly, even when I tried to share my excitement with him. I had woken up the morning of the birth and had signs of labour. I gave birth to a baby girl some eight hours later. It was a difficult delivery as the baby's shoulders were impacted in my pelvis. When we arrived at the hospital my contractions were very close, and extremely intense. I looked to George for comfort and support, which he was not only unable to offer me, he ridiculed and told me how ugly I looked. When our daughter was born he couldn't hide the disappointment from his face, as he felt pressure from his father to produce a son and carry on the family name. The doctor said, "Congratulations you have a baby girl, she weights 8lb 3oz and is 51cm. The baby has an erbs palsy".

I wondered what that meant, as I had never heard of the term before. I kept the baby in my hospital bed all night. I was so happy to have her in my life. The next morning when I unwrapped her from her clothing her arm just hung, it was lifeless. I frantically called for the nurse telling her there was something wrong with my baby's arm, to which she replied, "Your baby has an erbs palsy".

I asked, "What does that mean?"

She said, "The baby's arm is paralysed but will probably recover within two weeks".

I asked my gynaecologist and the paediatrician to explain this to me, as I didn't understand. They told me that most cases recover within two weeks, but that it was a case of wait and see. I was very distressed and I needed to talk to George. When he arrived at the hospital and I told him about the baby, he told me that it was my fault. He blamed me for our child's condition. There was a possibility that the baby would recover and I didn't want to worry my family unnecessarily, so I kept this to myself. Her condition took a lot longer to recover and I eventually let our family know. No one ever asked me how she was progressing and no one ever discussed it. Emotional support was non-existent in our family.

The first step is to know what to look for in a relationship whether romantic, platonic or professional.

How satisfied are you with your relationships?

Do you know what you want from relationships or do you just gravitate toward people or situations based on your story and patterns?

What are you willing or not willing to negotiate so that you do not compromise your values?

Chapter 3

Suffering is the Absence of Self Love

I prayed to God for our little girl to recover and promised never to complain about my life, thinking this was a sign that I should be more grateful. I focused on our little girl and put my own needs and our marital problems on the back burner once again. Seven months later I fell pregnant to twins. When I told George, his reaction was that he didn't want me to tell anyone that it was a twin pregnancy. Thinking back, I can only imagine that it was because his mother had lost twins at birth. Perhaps he felt it would bring bad luck if we told people. Although I so desperately wanted to share my news with my family I didn't question his wishes.

The twins were born six weeks early. With the added responsibility that comes with newborns my own health continued to deteriorate. Pushing my own needs down even further and focusing on gratitude. I had three beautiful children to love but as any mother knows having children so close in age without support is not an easy task. My days were filled with constantly attending to my growing family's needs.

I continued to ensure that my home and my children were always immaculate. Meals were always cooked for my family, I was usually too exhausted and distressed to eat. I didn't know what it meant to care for myself or my feelings even though my body was screaming for attention by way of physical pain. I tried to reach out to George for help and he would laugh at me and tell me that I was doing a good job on my own. He continued to ignore me until the situation became so unbearable that I told him I was leaving him. I recall he went into the kitchen and opened the cutlery drawer. He came over to me and stood centimetres away from my face with his hands behind his back holding something. He asked, "What did you say?". I was petrified, thinking he had a knife and was going to stab me for threatening to leave him. Fearing for my life I told him I didn't mean it.

George kept telling me that I was crazy, so I decided that if I was, I needed someone who was qualified to tell me that so I arranged an appointment with a psychiatrist. I was desperate for someone to listen to me; I wasn't coping and I had three toddlers who relied solely on me. Upon reflection I was probably struggling with post-natal depression whilst dealing with a mentally unstable husband and all of my own emotional baggage.

I decided to reach out to George's sister and tell her what was happening. We were not close but I thought she may be able to offer some insight into his behaviour. She seemed concerned and offered to come to the psychiatrist appointment with me. When I was called into the office, as I opened up to this stranger, I was too ashamed to look at him and tell him about my personal life. I stared at the wall instead as I opened up and told him everything that went on in my marriage. The trauma that occurred in the marital bedroom, the verbal abuse and the threats to kill me if I spoke to anyone.

George would threaten to kill me and bury me under the lemon tree in our backyard. I recall the doctor telling me that he had never met anyone who had been through such a dark period in their life, yet could articulate it so clearly. I told him that I wanted to help my husband and needed his guidance to do this. I was told that from what I had described, my husband was suffering from a number of mental health issues for which he needed to seek help. I was advised that for my own mental health I needed to remove myself from the situation. When my appointment was over, my sister-in-law was waiting for me.

As I stood there crying, I told her that I was leaving George. She hugged me and we both cried. In the following weeks, I left my marriage and my entire family turned their back on me. I tried to reach out to my sister-in-law and she told me that her loyalty was with her brother so she couldn't be there for me. I found myself totally alone and isolated. The stress of the separation and my own health issues had become so unbearable that I often wished I was dead. But who would take care of my children if I didn't exist?

One day when I was out with the children feeling unable to cope, I thought about crashing the car to escape my suffering. In my distress I chose to instead drive to a psychiatric hospital. I went to reception and told the man that I needed help, so they took the children from me and led me to a room. Not long after, another doctor came into the room and they listened to me for some time as I told them how I was feeling.

After a while they told me that I just needed someone to talk to and sent me home with a referral to a psychologist. Unexpectedly, one day my sister-in-law's husband came to my home to see me and the children. When he was leaving he hesitated and then told me that he was in love with me. I told him that he was confusing his feelings for the friendship we had developed, whilst being married into the same family. He had always been easy to get along with and always showed a special interest in my children.

When I later thought about what he had told me, I was confused. I mentioned this to my therapist and she asked why I found it difficult to believe that someone was attracted to me. I told her that it had more to do with the fact that we had both married into the same family. His name was Nick; he continued to pursue me, sending gifts to my home and place of work. He would also visit my children at school and take gifts to them. I told him that I could not be intimately involved with him as we were related through marriage. Nick asked if he could accompany me at my next psychologist appointment. He told the therapist that his marriage had been over for a long time and that he was leaving his wife. He said that he was genuine and wanted a relationship with me.

I was vulnerable and although I wasn't attracted to him, he had thrown me a lifeline when everyone else had turned their back on me. I developed an affection for him as he was kind to me and my children and we started dating. My love for him did grow over the years but I would often tell friends that I wouldn't have chosen him as my partner if my life situation was different. My family eventually got over the fact that I had left my husband and now had an issue with the fact that I was with Nick. The reality is that I could never be good enough in my family's eyes. Nick and I separated amicably many years later – he continues to have a relationship with my children and grandchildren who all adore him.

The human family I found myself in, is where I learned my values and my beliefs, these became my guide for life. And like my mother, I had somehow found myself with a man who verbally abused me and threatened to kill me. And even though my mother had experienced abuse, she told me that if a man wasn't an alcoholic, didn't gamble or run around with other women, he was a good husband. She didn't want me to leave my husband because of the shame and guilt she experienced when she left her husband.

She did everything in her power to ensure I stayed with George, including telling my extended family not to support me so that I would be forced to stay with him. Everyone has their own difficulties but dysfunctional people are not limited to alcoholism or what my mother described. I now see how her fears, lack of parenting skills and limiting beliefs drove her to make poor choices. She then passed those beliefs onto her children believing she was doing the right thing.

Many of us come from a place where we experienced abuse, neglect or suffered from trauma, whether real or perceived. And yet, that was our family, the people we loved and the ones who we thought would keep us safe, we looked to them for guidance. No matter how well intended, the best that parents ever provide is a mix of strength and frailty, wisdom and stupidity, good and bad choices and advice.

As the children of dysfunctional families, we were either never allowed or encouraged to express ourselves, our feelings or our fears. Hence we have a tendency to grow up feeling unworthy, unlovable, and to put it simply, "we never feel good enough". We learned to cope, to adapt to our feelings of shame from inherited values and belief which had nothing to do with us, or who we were born to be. I now have a greater level of awareness and can look back and appreciate that as humans, we are all perfectly imperfect.

My life journey took me to levels of darkness where I lost parts of my soul. Yet our soul never gives up on us, it gives us signs, forever guiding us to find our way back. It presents situations to us, makes us feel uncomfortable as it nudges us to find our way back to ourselves. For this to happen, we must be brave enough to make changes and to grow. We must learn to be in tune with ourselves, to face our fears, trust ourselves and our inner knowing. Always be open to learn and to move toward our purpose rather that remain in a place of fear and victim mentality, even if it means letting people and material things go. I feel blessed for the journey which led me to the teachings of amazing spiritual healers such as: Dr Joe Dispenza, Dr John Demartini, Dr Wayne Dyer, Louise Hay, Eckhart Tolle, Deepak Chopra, Brene Brown, to name a few. This spiritual journey contributed to my personal growth, helping me to clarify my values and beliefs and as a consequence my own healing.

Self-love is more than just being good to ourselves by soaking in a hot bath or having a massage. These things are nice but self-love is an inner job, it means creating a better relationship with you, treating yourself with kindness and compassion and realising that you have a right to be happy.

What part of you have you been ignoring because you are busy building an empire, raising a family or living up to all of your shoulds, which have been instilled into you by society, your parents or old versions of yourself?

Chapter 4

Shifting From Victim to Power

One day when I was at my psychotherapy appointment, I was describing how difficult life had become. I was so tired that I was considering giving in, and going back to my husband. I recall the therapist saying, "That would be like going back to bondage". I was so naive, I didn't even really know what that meant. I thought about those words and wondered, *was it really that bad?* I mean, you only know what you know, right? Growing up I was not allowed to have friends as my parents believed they would be a bad influence.

I didn't know life outside of my own family, hence I went from a controlling family to a controlling husband. I had never experienced independence.

After separating from my husband, in an attempt to have some social interaction and meet new people, I decided to join the local YMCA where they provided childcare with an annual membership. I didn't have a lot of money, but I made this happen, and I was able to get some respite. I was able to participate in group fitness classes, whilst my children were cared for. I continued to invest in my personal development and with the help of my therapist, I continued to work on my limiting beliefs. Eventually, I managed to stand on my own two feet and found a way to live beyond my story. I wanted to give myself and my children a chance to break the cycle that my therapist described as "bondage".

When I say, 'I chose to stand on my own two feet,' I need to tell you that often I stumbled and I fell. There were so many times that I would find myself in a deep dark place, where I could hardly see the light. I stumbled in the darkness as I held my children close, protecting and guiding them with everything I had left in me. I created an image in my mind of my children hanging off a cliff, and the amount of strength I needed to hold onto them, so they wouldn't fall. That image not only helped me to hold onto my life, it helped me to keep going. Letting go was not an option with that image in mind.

I gained the realisation very early on that my children did not ask for this situation. I wanted to give them a safer, more loving childhood than my own. I buried all of my wishes and desires and focused on their welfare. Only in recent years, have I been able to make sense of my life and find gratitude in my journey. This isn't to say that the traumatic events of my childhood were acceptable. Every child deserves to be loved and protected, both physically and emotionally. It's a realisation, that my parents loved me in the best way they knew how. More importantly, I now choose to see myself as worthy and loveable. I now see that they were incapable of parenting any differently, nor were they able to completely heal themselves from their past. I can also now see that they were seeking love and acceptance just as much as I was. I could finally see how we inherit from our past, values and beliefs that limit us from truly living our purpose.

It's an awakening that each of us is responsible for our choices as we journey through our own personal growth. To blame our past for our current situation, only serves to limit us further. I believe that the purpose of our life is to seek to grow and evolve. As children we were not able to change our situation, but at some point we must make a choice. As adults, we can only be held back by our own fear. But in order for something to be a choice, we must allow it to come into our awareness and we must be willing to accept the uncomfortable emotions that come up in the process of healing. There is truth in the saying, "When the student is ready the teacher appears" – Lao Tzu.

To escape any situation we are unhappy about, we must be brave enough to make changes and to grow. We must learn to be in tune with ourselves, to face our fears, trust ourselves and our inner knowing.

Always be open to learn and to move toward our purpose rather than remain in a place of fear and victim mentality. As Dr Joe Dispenza says, "You literally have to become someone else as you cannot create a new reality with the same personality."

The moment I was able to find gratitude for the lessons I learned along the way, was when I was able to set myself free. Free from my past, to live in the moment where I am able to choose how I live the rest of my life. With a sense of gratitude to guide me, I am able to choose my thoughts, instead of my thoughts controlling me. My journey and all of my life experiences have led me to become the woman I am today. I like her, I fought to become her and I am glad I believed in her.

When Dr Wayne Dyer passed away they released the movie *The Shift*, in his memory. It was after watching *The Shift* that I remembered my deep love for writing. The very next day I walked into a local St Vinnies store where I was drawn to a writing desk! It felt like the universe just placed it there for me – as I laid eyes on it I was drawn to it. I felt mesmerized as I approached it, in what felt like slow motion. I instantly fell in love with it. I had to have it. It belonged to me and I belonged to it. I sat at my newly acquired desk every day, yet the words just didn't flow.

Not long after that after yet another failed relationship, I sold my home, and the desk, and forgot about my writing once again.

At this point I had given up on myself, of ever finding happiness. I had nothing left to give and nothing to look forward to. What was the point of this life, living in misery and continuous struggle? Sinking back into the familiar dark place, I was incapable of working. I lived off the proceeds of the sale of my home wishing my life away, hoping my funds would last until retirement age. It was during this time that I met my coach and mentor. I decided to participate in his training courses which led me to deeper levels of self-discovery.

After completing his numerous personal development courses and attaining my certification as an Emotional Freedom Technique practitioner I continued to work with my mentor. Together we did the deep work required to clear my childhood traumas, which had negatively affected all areas of my life.

I was not only able to re-enter the workplace, I was promoted within six months of commencing work. It's ironic where life takes us, how it presents opportunities for us to grow when we allow our minds to be in the moment. Breaking the chains from our past to create something new was not an easy road but one that is definitely worthwhile.

As a child I did not have the resources that I needed to change my circumstances. I haven't been that child for a long, long time, and yet I continued to suffer from my past many years later. I continued to seek the love and approval from people who were simply incapable of giving it to themselves, let alone give it to me!

Often we are afraid to let go of an idea of how things are supposed to be. It takes courage to give up on something you once believed in, but sometimes it's necessary if you want to move on.

With the knowledge that allowing our mind to keep repeating the stories of our past we experience the same painful emotions over and over again. With this in mind, how can you heal your emotional wounds from the past?

Dad bottle feeding piglets at our home in Cyprus

Dad proud of crop produced on our citrus farm (pictured left to right) Dad, Aunt Anastasia, paternal grandmother & mum

Me & Mum - Australia 1965

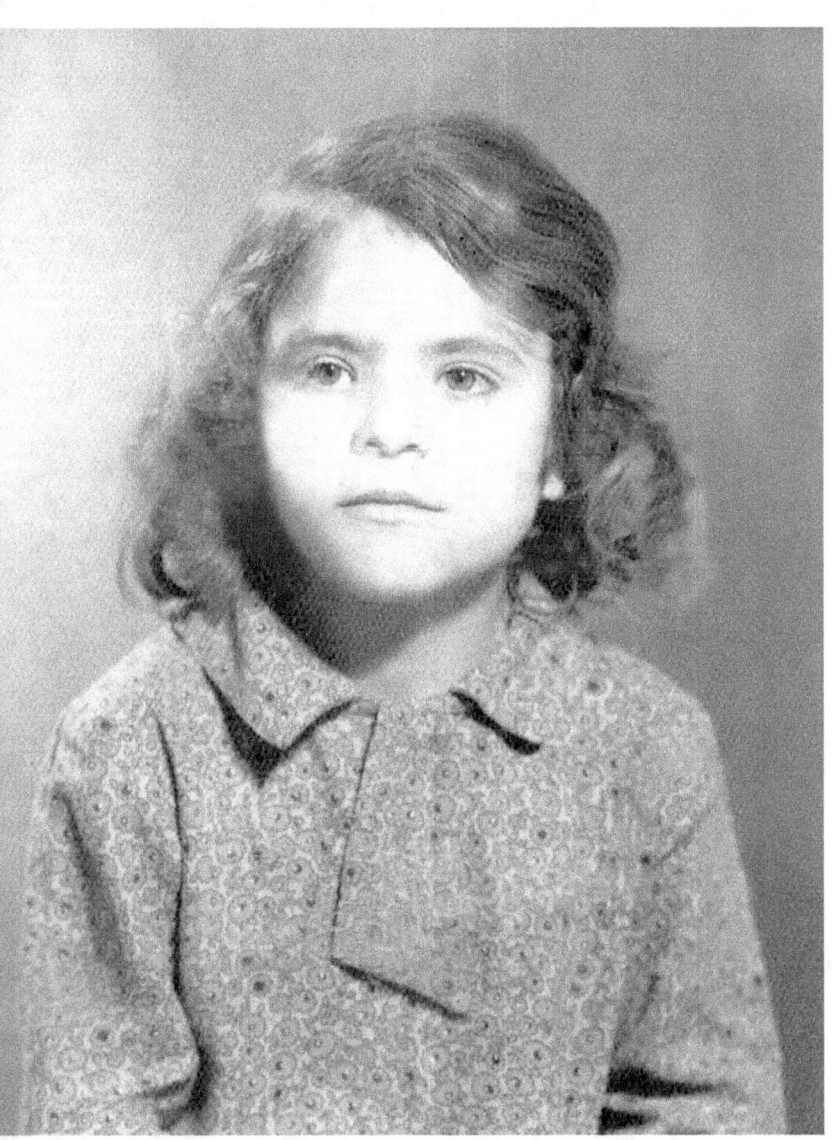

Me (passport photo) 1965

Dad & Mum - Cyprus 1951

Mum age 39

Miscellaneous family pic

Dad in his sewing room age 93

Ruins of our home in Achna Cyprus 2006

Mum, Me & Dad 2016

Mum & Me having lunch for my 50th birthday

Nicole, Anadele, Me (age 27) & James

Chapter 5

Let Go and Grow

Recognising that we were starved from the love and affection we needed as children is an important first step to recovery. Our emotional needs may not have been met in infancy, childhood or adolescence. We may have been deprived of love in the past but what we learned about love in childhood can be unlearned. We can make a choice *to let go and grow!*

To put an end to suffering and to be happy we must realise who we are beyond our history and our life situations. We must forgive those who caused us pain and realise that their actions were dictated by limiting conditions created by the particular culture they were born and raised in, or they may not have had the language to describe what they felt or needed.

It is a profound moment in our lives when we can let go of the past and surrender to something bigger. Living every day to the fullest knowing that we are all perfectly imperfect and worthy of love.

My compassion and love for the little girl inside of me was awakening for the first time. As I re-parent and hold that little girl close to me, nurturing, supporting and loving her unconditionally, together we continue this journey called life. A renewed commitment to my life purpose and my dreams. Using the wisdom, gratitude, compassion and learnings that I now have to let go of the emotional baggage my inner child brought into adulthood.

I continue to invest in my self-development, and in the process I have met some amazing like-minded people, who have encouraged and supported my journey.

These days I am committed to my well-being and in doing so I am balanced, centred and focused. Having redefined my values and beliefs that are in line with who I truly am, has awakened the writer in me, who I had lost for over four decades.

I woke up one day last week and the words were alive in my head, so I decided to put them on paper. In the past few weeks whenever I feel inspired, I write and the words flow naturally from within. At first, I had no idea where they came from but it felt as though someone opened up the gates and set my soul free. My writing feels like it comes from a place of inner stillness. Detaching from my ego, from myself, who I thought I was or had to be, has set me free to be me. Letting go of our personal history – the events of our past – and allowing ourselves to live in the present moment allows us to return to our true selves, to set our soul free.

We can only experience this freedom when we are ready for this change. I continue to invest in myself without feeling guilty and for no other reason other than because I deserve my love just as much as anyone else. It is not selfish to nourish your soul, it is necessary. I sometimes wish that I had discovered the art of healing myself from my past earlier, but I guess I wouldn't be who I am today.

My life, my happiness, my creativity and the relationships with my chosen loved ones is so much more rewarding. I no longer feel the pain from my past, burn out and resentment, that we feel when we have lost ourselves. When we don't acknowledge our emotions, when we are not being true to ourselves and instead turn to self-medicating with alcohol, drugs, or seeking self-worth from something else outside of who we are we stop ourselves from finding the happiness we deserve.

The Buddha defines enlightenment as "the end of suffering". Rather than wait for this, that, or something else to happen before you are happy or at peace, you will learn to find it exactly where it has always been, inside yourself.

I now support others to reconnect with themselves so they can find their way back to themselves. To find peace, joy and happiness, good health, feeling confident in their body, creativity – these are just some of the side benefits that happen naturally when we find ourselves and set our soul free.

May you find your way back to yourself so that you can enjoy all of life's gifts.

Stella x

To let go of past hurts, you need to make a conscious decision to take control of your life and your situation. Forgiveness and gratitude are vital to the healing process because they allow you to let go of anger, guilt, shame, sadness, or any other emotion you may be experiencing and move on.

What hurts are you still holding onto that are stopping you from being happy?

A Poetic Reflection

Expressing Life Through Verses

These verses are a reflection of my life experiences. I invite you into my thoughts and my feelings as I share with you the lessons I have learnt. May you enjoy reading them as much as I have enjoyed writing them.

BORN TO BE ME

As I awake, and take a breath.
A brand new day now lays ahead.
No then, no when just here and now.
I could begin if I knew how.

Instead of breaking my habits old.
Those beliefs that I've been told.
I keep them close they are my truth.
But in my heart this was uncouth.

I am a girl who came to earth.
My life began like any birth.
The issue is they had a past.
And in themselves they did not trust.

Their egos bigger than their hearts.
Do this not that! each day they'd blast.
I tried so hard just to be me.
My soul seeking just to be free.

The years went by then I began.
To question truths that I now had.
The mould then did begin to break.
And it was not without heartache.

For being me meant I would lose.
The human family I did choose.
So torn between being me and them.
So intertwined where does this end?

I tried instead to find this me.
That I was told that I should be.
And every task I took to hand.
I would complete until the end.

For I have pride I told myself.
I must lay low don't make a sound.
Just follow in the path that led.
To all the dreams of me they had.

This could not last for it's not me.
And so my soul I need to see.
For all the love the joy I seek.
Is flowing through now as I speak.

Although I'm older I'm still me.
My soul screaming just to be free.
My dreams my hopes it's my journey.
It's up to me to set me free.

IN LOVING MEMORY OF MY FATHER

Three years today since Dad has passed.
And I can say, all's in the past.
I do not bear a lasting grudge.
About all things me, that he did judge.

I must be who he thought he bred.
With this I battled in my head.
I tried so hard to be the one.
Who he would praise, who he would love.

I followed him around all day.
In hope, in vain that he would say.
Come sit with me I want to know.
What do you seek, or need to grow.

And as we battled with no words.
We built a bridge with pride and hurts.
If only then we'd paused awhile.
To lift the veil instead of bail.
We would have seen we're both the same.
It's love we seek, we're all humane.
But those beliefs that we picked up.
Led us astray, we grew apart.

We missed the chance to get to know.
Each other's soul remained unknown.
And so today I want to say.
Don't let your words get in the way.

For those we love they come and go.
For me and Dad, we were too slow.
Yet Dad lives on inside my heart.
Eternal souls can't be apart.

And in my dreams, he came to say.
You were so loved in my own way.
I could not show, I could not speak.
The love I now know that you seek.
It was in vain, it seems insane.
So reach out don't you miss that train.
Don't wait to make up in your dreams.
Although it's never too late it seems.

A wise man Marshall Rosenberg.
Opened my eyes to endless truth.
So go ahead and get his book.
Find common ground with friend or foe.
Let's end the hurt as we all grow.

Written by me in loving memory of the amazing soul I chose as my father for this soul journey – inspired by Marshall Rosenberg PhD

LET GO OF BLAME

When once a child I had big dreams.
My future bright or so it seemed.
My wisdom young as were my years.
Yet I had cried so many tears.

I could not bear heartache to see.
There was great love inside of me.
So I would try to make mum laugh.
When I could see that life was tough.

So I took sides to rescue her.
Dad beat her so, I did choose her.
I once heard screams it was my knowing.
Impending troubles were a brewing.

So I did faint in front of him.
Tried to distract Dad from his sin.
The years did pass as did the days.
Tried to forget his brutal ways.

Along the way we get confused.
For the word love is loosely used.
You either care or you do not.
When you decide to tie the knot.

I think it's right it should be law.
A rearing class we should partake.
Before allowed to consummate.
Parenting sure, it isn't new.
But Many most don't have a clue.

Parents unknowingly hurt their young.
For a child's mind is like a sponge.
The angry words that they do hear.
They often stick don't disappear.

We spend our lives trying to work out.
Why our own thoughts we often doubt.
Because our minds our self-esteem.
Is often buried deep within.

It takes some time it takes deep work.
To break the chain and heal the hurt.
So use your brain don't you refrain.
To grow we must let go of blame.

MY FAMILY TREE

I fell in love, or so I thought.
One that aligned with what was taught.
Or better still what I did see.
One that came from my family tree.

For what we learn as we do grow.
All that we see all that we know.
Is what our mum or dad display.
It was not planned it's come what may.

They learned it too it's all they knew.
The questions then they were too few.
That was just life way back when.
No internet or great big plan.

The village folk they were confined.
By their old rules they were defined.
To old thinking they didn't dare.
To bend the rules their souls to bare.

Their childhood dreams they put away.
As they were told that they'd bring shame.
To all before them who denied.
All their big dreams for the family name.

So who are you to question this.
To break away will you find peace?
What do you seek what will you find?
Are you unsure don't feel aligned?

All that you know is that in life.
You have a chance to shine your light.
And to have lived this you must do.
To your own self you must be true.

INHERITED VALUES & BELIEFS

Every generation blames the one before.
These words I know you've heard somewhere.
As they're now in a song.
For all of us who can relate.

Of values and beliefs.
That someone somewhere handed us.
They lay them at our feet.
They then became our guide for life.

I'm sure you would agree.
The thoughts we have inside our head.
Come from our family tree.
We may dispute, or think they're cute.

They form just who we are.
We instantly react from there.
And often take us far.
From where we thought our path would lead.

They bring us much despair.
If in our minds we do believe.
The world just doesn't care.
If they forever challenge us.
Then you must take the reins.

To choose beliefs that serve your soul.
And give you back your light.
It's time for you to take control.
And own it with delight.

For future generations, will benefit from thee.
When you ignite your spark your light.
You set you, and them free.

FINDING OUR WAY BACK HOME

When once a child, born wild and free.
I was happy, as I could see.
The world as is, the fresh cool breeze.
And all the joy, life really is.

And day by day, faded away.
The memory of being born to play.
As all around the angry sound.
Of all life's' woes from friends and foes.

Began to seep inside of me.
Into my world began to creep.
A point of view, that made me blue.
It whispered things, that were not true.

For now I know, nor friend or foe.
Can give or take the life I make.
It's up to me, to now break free.
To carve a path that lets me see.

And this does mean that I must choose.
Which of the humans I may lose.
As people come into our lives.
They are life's' lessons in disguise.

Yet we hold on, choose not to grow.
Because we want the life we know.
It's fear that leads us to all pain.
For so much more, we have to gain.

Yet we can't see that it is we.
Holding on to the family tree.
Instead of blossom as we must.
Free to live life, with joy and trust.

About the Author

Stella Georgiou is an ICF (International Coaching Federation) Certified Results Coach & EFT practitioner with over fifteen years' experience in the Fitness Industry working as a Personal Coach. She is the mother of three adult children and two grandchildren.

She is the founder of STELLAResults Wellness / Mindset Coaching where she supports people to navigate life's emotional challenges enabling them to find the happiness they seek.

Her passion for healing comes from having herself experienced childhood trauma, which affected many areas of her life including her physical and mental health. Her treating doctor told her many years ago that the damage to her nervous system due to the trauma she had experience could never be healed. Despite this she believed there was more to her than her life experiences. She continued to search for what she knew deep down was her birth right.

She has overcome the limiting beliefs from her past, enabling her to heal herself, and to live a happy and fulfilling life.

Stella now helps others to identify what is keeping them stuck so they can improve their emotional and physical health and move to a place of peace, joy and happiness.

Recommended Resources

Books

- Nonviolent Communication - Marshall B Rosenberg, PhD – PuddleDancer Press
- The Power of Now – Echhart Tolle – Namaste Publishing
- Creating Mindful Moments – Sandra Harwood – Busy Bird Publishing
- Excuses Begone – Dr Wayne W Dyer – Hay House Authors

- I can see clearly now – Dr Wayne W Dyer – Hay House Authors
- You Can Heal Your Life – Louis Hay – Hay House
- The Gifts of Imperfection – Dr Brene Brown – Research Professor

Audio Books

- The Body Keeps the Score - (Brain & Trauma) By -Bessel Van Der Kolk
- Falling into Grace – Insights to end suffering Adyashanti
- The Top Five Regrets of the Dying – Bronnie Ware
- Becoming Supernatural – Dr Joe Dispenza
- The Biology of Belief – Dr Bruce Lipton

Websites

- https://www.drwaynedyer.com/ Dr Wayne W Dyer – Self-Help Author / Speaker
- https://www.louisehay.com/ Louise Hay – Spiritual Healer
- https://drjoedispenza.com/ Dr Joe Dispenza – Neuroscientist
- https://www.cnvc.org/ Marshall B Rosenberg, PhD
- https://www.brucelipton.com/ Dr Bruce Lipton PhD
- https://brenebrown.com/ Brene Brown

TED Talks/Videos/YouTube

- https://www.ted.com/talks/brene_brown_on_vulnerability/up-next
- https://www.youtube.com/watch?v=DeVGLQw_Zdk

- https://www.youtube.com/watch?v=7xmGi9UzVIY
- https://www.youtube.com/watch?v=VT8KGgDo6TY

App

Calm: Meditation to Relax, Focus & Sleep Better available on the App Store & Google Play, compatible with Android and OS devices

Thank you!

To encourage you on your journey my gifts to you if you choose are:

- One week free yoga
  – Oshun Yoga Retreat
- One week free Zoom exercise classes
  – Unique Wellness
- Free Discovery Session
  – STELLAResults Coaching

You Can Book Your Gifts by visiting the sites below:

- Meditation – Oshun Yoga / Meditation / Pilates https://www.oshunretreat.com.au/
- Personal Coach / Exercise / Wellness https://uniqueptwellness.com/
- Personal Coach / Wellness / Mindset www.stellaresultscoaching.com.au

NOTES

www.ingramcontent.com/pod-product-compliance
Lightning Source LLC
Chambersburg PA
CBHW071518080526
44588CB00011B/1472